THIS BOOK
BELONGS TO

....

INSTRUCTIONS

 Turn off the distractions around you and relax.

 Have fun! There is no wrong way to color, and with this book you are is sure to have hours of relaxation and enjoyment.

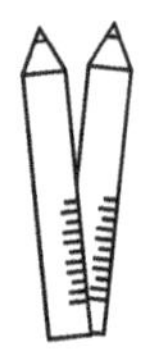 This book works best with color pencils or markers. Wet mediums might bleed through. As images are printed one side only, you may place a piece of paper or card if you notice bleed through.

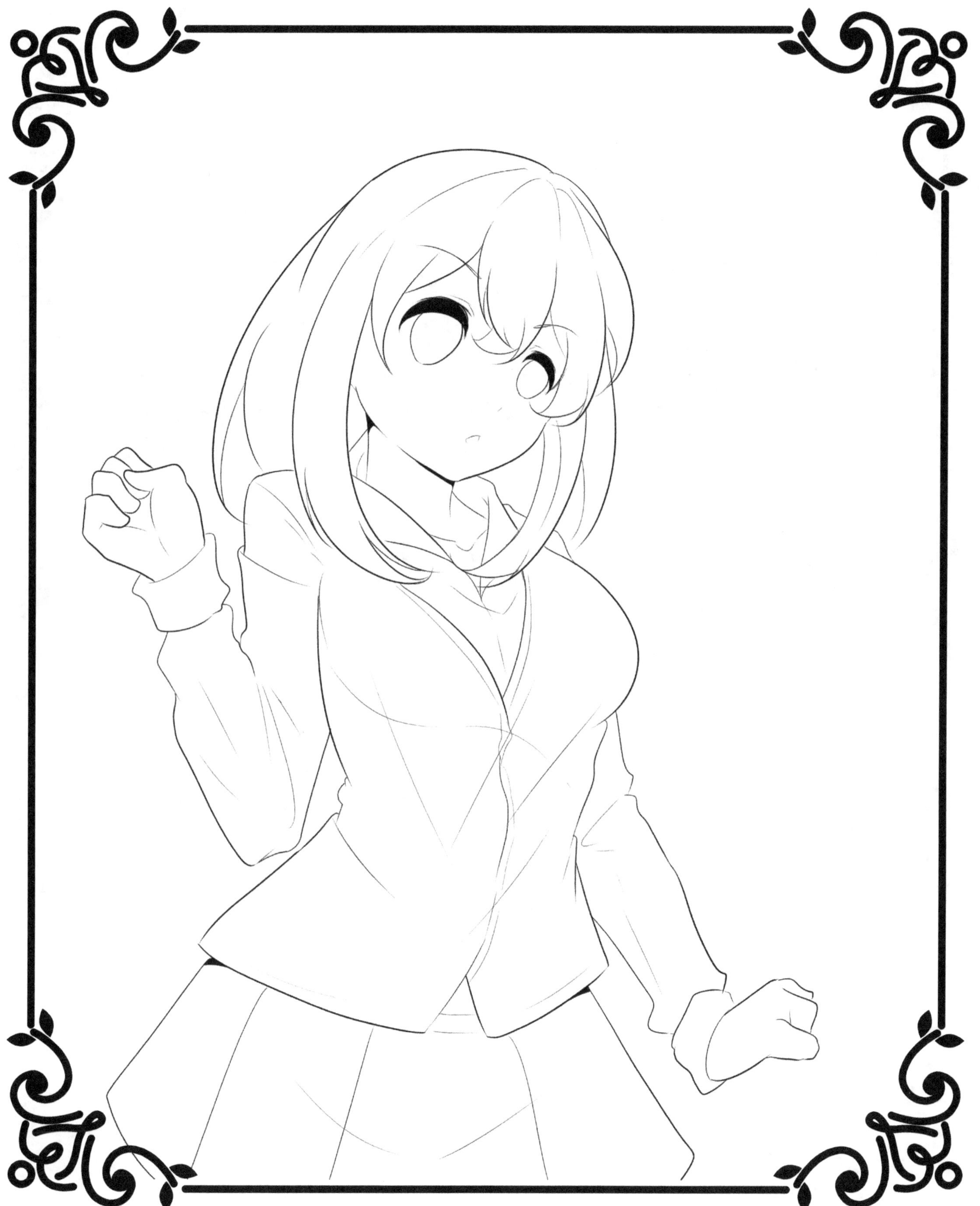

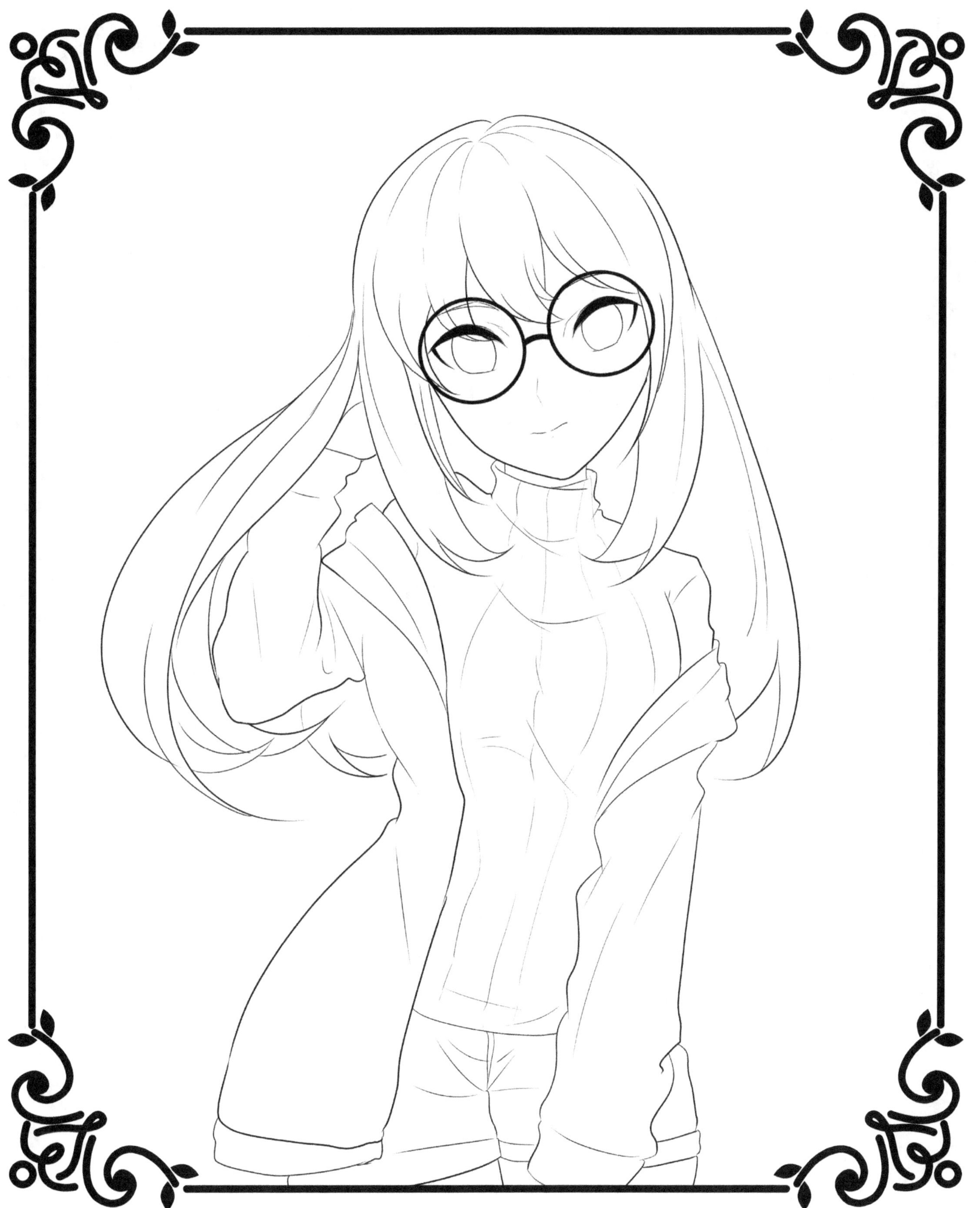